No Hurry

Also by Michael Blumenthal

Sympathetic Magic: Poems

Days We Would Rather Know: Poems

Laps: A Book-Length Poem

Against Romance: Poems

To Woo and To Wed: Poets on Love and Marriage (editor)

Weinstock Among the Dying: A Novel

When History Enters the House: Central European Essays, 1992-1996

Dusty Angel: Poems

And Yet: Selected Poems of Péter Kántor (editor and translator)

All My Mothers and Fathers: A Memoir

Correcting the World: Selected Poetry and Writings of Michael Blumenthal

And: Poems

Unknown Places: Poems by Péter Kántor (translator)

No Hurry

Poems 2000–2012

Michael Blumenthal

etruscan press

Etruscan Press
Wilkes University
84 West South Street
Wilkes-Barre, PA 18766
(570) 408-4546

WILKES UNIVERSITY

www.etruscanpress.org

Published 2012 by Etruscan Press
Printed in the United States of America
Design by Julianne Popovec
Cover photograph by Michael Blumenthal
The text of this book is set in Electra Std.

First Edition

12 13 14 15 16 5 4 3 2 1

Library of Congress Cataloging-in-Publication Data

Blumenthal, Michael.
      No hurry : poems 2000-2012 / Michael Blumenthal. -- 1st ed.
      p. cm.
   ISBN 978-0-9832944-7-4 (acid-free paper)
   I. Title.
   PS3552.L849N64 2012
   811'.54--dc23

Please turn to the back of this book for a list of the sustaining funders of Etruscan Press.

This book is printed on recycled, acid-free paper.

for my colleagues at the West Virginia University College of Law who, blessedly, have been in no hurry to send me away

HURRY UP PLEASE ITS TIME
If you don't like it you can get on with it, I said,
Others can pick and choose if you can't.

—T.S. Eliot, "The Waste Land"

He noted with curiosity that there seemed to be no
hurry, that there was all the time in the world, time to
take account of small events in the garage.

—Walker Percy, *The Second Coming*

If you're Larkin or Bishop, one book a decade is enough. If you're
not? More than enough.

—James Richardson, *Vectors*

No Hurry

Acknowledgments

The author wishes to thank the editors of the following publications, in which certain poems in this manuscript originally appeared. Some of these works have been edited somewhat since the time of their original publication:

The Academy of American Poets (www.poets.org)
"The Nurse"

The American Scholar
"Not the Soul"

Chelsea
"Because Marriage Is Not for Romantics"
"Samizdat's Muse"

Connotation Press
"What Happened?"
"Self-Help"
"Everyone Is Wonderful When They're Wonderful"

Crazyhorse
"The Past"
"Motel on the Mountain"

The Cortland Review
"Madden's Pond"
"Written on the Day After My Sister's Death"
"The End of Sex"
"Blessed"
"No Hurry"

Five A.M.
"And the Fish Swim in the Lake, And Do Not Even Own Clothing"

Green Mountain Review
"Virtue"
"The Other Side of the Story"
"I Died"

Legal Studies Forum
"The Wounded"
"Abstractions"

New Letters
"Two Short"
"The Pigeon"

The New Republic
"The Human Condition"
"Be Kind"

New Works Review
"Weeping at the Oscars"
"For My Son, Reading *Harry Potter*"
"For Grief Will Ultimately Have Its Way"

Nightsun
"Lilac Nostalgia"
"Anthology"

Onyx 3
"A Photo of Terezin"
"*Le Choix*"

Poetry
"I Think Constantly of Those Who Were Truly Great"

Poetry Porch
"In a Time of Economic Downturn, I Gaze Up at the Sky"
"Redundancies of Evening"
"Background Music"

"Hypochondria"
"Poetry Love"
"Nostalgia for Paris"

Portfolio Weekly (**VA**)
"Virtue"

Prairie Schooner
"The Rabbi Writes a Marriage Poem"
"Homage to Charles Aznavour"

Princeton University Library Journal
"Habitations"

Santa Clara Magazine
"Two Arts"

Seattle Review
"Six Cheerful Couplets on Death"

The Southern Review
"Desire"
"Here Is Your Striped Shirt"
"God's Window"

The Southwest Review
"Atelier Rheingold"

T88, A Journal
"Civic Leaders"
"The Germans"

Valparaiso Poetry Review
"Autobiography of a Face"

Author's Note

When one publishes a collection of poems written over some fifteen years, one inevitably invokes a past that no longer exists, along with the self—invariably changed itself—that inhabited it. Many of the poems contained herein are products of such a past time, written by a person who, while I do not wish to disavow his existence, I (gratefully) no longer entirely am. I have included whatever poems are the product of such a self because they still speak to me—and, hopefully, will to the reader as well—as poems, rather than as bits of autobiographical "data." And it is as poems that I hope, and trust, they will be read—designed, as I feel poems should be, to provide pleasure and solace, rather than information, tracing the evolution of years that, as life must be, are forever changing, while holding to the enduring imperatives of this sometimes sullen but always pleasure-producing art.

No Hurry

1. Mixed Blessings

Depending which comes first and most
The lightning or the rain
Will dictate how the souls of men
Will cleanse or turn profane

—Sally Harper Bates, "Mixed Blessings"

Atelier Rheingold

Berlin, January 2000

Here is a room
where, for two hundred Deutschmarks and a smile,
you can be tied, in a plastic or a rubber suit,
to a beautiful cage and be beaten
or kicked, stepped-on, role-played
into oblivion, where everything
that can never be yours at home
can finally be yours, in which
you can be Salvador Dali in red tights
or Dracula in black, or the Count
of Monte Cristo riding a wild horse
(named Eszter or Monica, as you choose),
or even, once again, the Lone Ranger
in his sweet black mask. You can be
a beaten bundle of whimpering flesh,
a master, a slave, a circus of needs
that, for a price, some sweet young girl
will seek to satisfy, sending you home
to your ordinary life once more, a little
less needy, perhaps a little less in love.

And here is another room —
"the clinic," as they say —
in which you can play "Doctor"
one more time, now with a paid nurse
dressed in tights, or simply lie back
and let yourself be probed and penetrated

just like a child, with tools
and utensils too sterile to be true,
beneath loving fingers hired for a song
and mirrors of all kinds in which
to view yourself, relishing a pain
that hurts so good, as if it were
your destiny made new again.

And here is the last,
the simplest one of all,
resembling most of all the analyst's domain
(but for two mirrors slanted on the wall,
a single dildo, and these ropes of different shades)
with its rubber bed and glass of juice,
a good deal less expensive than the rest,
into which the merely miserable descend,
and where the able-bodied Paula comes,
bringing a relief both palpable and kind
from all the disappointments life can bring,
here in the well-presented *Atelier Rheingold*,
from which you exit once again
onto the undivided streets, a world
made whole again for just a fee,
a kindly universe where there's a cure
for every unlived fantasy a life provides,
chargeable to EuroCard, American Express,
with an e-mail address all its own,
just seconds from the U-Bahn each one takes
to get, in his own way, home again.

The Rabbi Writes a Marriage Poem

Because he is more devoted to the moral than the true,
the rabbi's poem turns constantly away
from its author's ambivalence, it turns constantly

toward a kind of stubborn devotion to his wife,
his children, the institution of marriage itself,
like a road headed steeply downhill that must pause

every few miles for a scenic outlook of some sort,
a consoling view that will allow the driver to go on,
to keep heading downhill, but not too fast, never

out of control, and so, whenever the word *desire*
rears its unruly head, it must be followed shortly
thereupon by *duty*, and, of course, *love*,

because the rabbi, after all, is in the love
and duty business, the rabbi is a pillar
of the community, and pillars must be solid,

steadfast, unswerving in their devotion to what is
righteous, even at the price of a certain infidelity
to the poem, whose business, after all, is to careen

wholeheartedly toward the truth—narrow, dark,
and deep—of what we feel indeed, but the rabbi
feels duty-bound to all that can be recited

from a podium, with conviction, to the assembled
faithful, the rabbi is heavy with the weight
of examples he must set for the more dangerously

poetic, so he takes out his eraser and, whenever,
he comes upon the word *lust*, substitutes *love*,
whenever there is a moment of *doubt*, he substitutes

faith, he wants to keep this poem of his from heading
downhill too fast, he knows a man can be wholeheartedly
devoted to only one thing, he has entered into this

workshop only on a whim, a kind of poetic aside
to his actual life, and so he applies the brakes,
he calls the poem to a halt at a dangerous turn,

an ungodly truth, a painful desire, as rabbis must.

A Photo of Terezin

for Linda Gregerson

And it may happen to a sweeper
as he waves
his dirty broom
about without a hope
among the dusty ruins
of a wasteful colonial exhibition
that he halts amazed
before a remarkable statue
of dried leaves and brooms
representing we believe
dreams
crimes celebrations lightning
and laughter again longing
trees and birds
also the moon and love and sun and death . . .

—Jacques Prévert

Because beauty has never been moral, though
the moral may, on occasion, be beautiful,
I stop in front of the sterilization vats, where

the lice- and disease-ridden clothes of the prisoners
were washed after a day of hard labor, and, because
I find the delicate pink-and-white colored walls,

the slightly oxidized gray, and the immaculate
ceramic white of the vats themselves
disconcertingly beautiful, I snap a picture

in memory of my father's brother Erwin, who died
fighting for the Germans in World War I, in memory
of his wicked stepmother Jeannette, gassed at

Buchenwald, and in memory of my beloved
grandmother Johanna, still brushing her black dress
the morning she had to leave her ancestral home

near Nuremberg forever, on this back-lit lovely day
in the Czech countryside, and I know that wherever
we find beauty needs to be praised, that even the young

Nazi soldier who paused for a moment while pushing
the young girl toward the gas chamber to admire
her loveliness, was not unredeemable — he, too,

may have found, later in life, some human redemption,
and, as I sit here now in the Hungarian countryside,
admiring this photo, I realize I have done right

to take it, that I will go to nearby Tapolca tomorrow
and have it blown up, then framed, and mount it
on the wall above my writing desk, I the offspring

of the persecuted and slaughtered, the betraying
and betrayed, so as to remind myself that beauty
is not so much selected as it selects, that the venues

of its kingdoms are neither righteous nor assured,
and that they can occur anywhere, my friend,
anywhere anywhere anywhere anywhere.

Lilac Nostalgia

for Patricia Hampl

There were pages of pictures of perfect cakes, and one was called Lilac Nostalgia. The picture had individual lilac blossoms frozen in sparkling sugar, as if in a deathless frost, each flower affixed to the cake all over like little lilac medallions. And home I went, set up my chem experiment in the kitchen. And I was deeply content painting dry egg white onto lilac blossoms and then raining superfine sugar on them and laying these sugar-drunk petals on parchment paper . . .

For Francois Mitterrand's last meal, it is rumored
the President began with oysters, flat *belons*,
not too salty, eating a dozen between spasms of pain,

then followed by *ortolans*, that finch-like bunting
from southwest France known for its tender flesh,
of which the President speared the last. In all,

the dying Mitterrand ate thirty oysters, some *foie gras*,
a slice of capon, that venerable chicken, and two
ortolans, before passing into history. We do not know

what the cancer-ridden man had for dessert, but I doubt
it was Lilac Nostalgia, though the sugar-drunk petals
would surely have pleased him. What I love most

about the French is that their hungers are apolitical,
that neither a man nor a woman need apologize
for what makes them human. It's easy to get sentimental

about lilacs, for example, to feel like an environmentalist
when a beautiful woman dips them in egg whites,
coats them with superfine sugar, and pins them, like

a lepidopterist, to a cake. Mitterrand, I'm sure, would
have loved them, though, in all likelihood, it was
a crème brûlée, or a *tarte aux pommes*, with which

he ended. Still, it's lovely to think of him dining that night
just as they did at Versailles, holding a small flowerlet
in his dying grasp, like a lover's hand, nostalgic already

for the pleasures of this life, unsure what perfections
the next one will bring, or whose hand it was
that had laid down those sugared stars.

Because Marriage Is Not for Romantics

we should meet in some Central European city
in June, when even the insects are mating
and all the bridges between the possible and impossible
are crowded with traffic, when the boats
are sailing down the Danube
as if it were the River of Forgetfulness
and there is no sin left to remain undiscovered,
only the loneliness of flesh humming
I am here, I am here, as if
it were the deep susurrus of the angels
who know better than we do
that all possibilities were created
for us to approach them
we who know in the end
that even the cities of the blessed
are places of sin and redemption,
that even the swan and the nightingale
must occasionally sing alone,
in the ravenous dark, a magical song
in praise of deceitfulness and passion
in praise of flowing waters
and those desperately beautiful bastions
of romance and desire and impossible love.

Le Choix

> *Il faux choisir: mourir ou mentir.* (One has to choose: to die or to lie . . .)

> —Céline, *Voyage au Bout de la Nuit*

The choice is always painful, never clear:
The devil choosing between kinds of death.
Il faut choisir: mourir, mentir.

The angels sing in riddles, ear to ear,
That lives expire while there still is breath
The choice is always painful, never clear.

Not every vow that's uttered can be dear:
The ache of marriage, and the salve of sex
Il faut choisir: mourir, mentir.

Those well-placed lies, emboldened cavaliers
Who come with kisses, flowers, songs, and yet
Still know the choice is painful, never clear.

I meet my love in secret, year to year
In hotel rooms and stations, *sans* regret,
I pay the price: *mourir, mentir.*

The puritanical of heart sometimes foreswear
The paltry pleasures others take for wealth
Il faut mentir, and then: *il faut mourir.*
The choice is always painful, and unclear.

Habitations

Austin, Texas, New Year's 2000

In each of these houses, a habitation,
and, in each habitation, lives
in the making, small orgies
of particulars and wildnesses,
where unto some a Saviour is born,
unto others a mere profligacy
of wishes, desires, habits,
oracles of turkey and dressing,
an abundance of stuffing and egg nog,
a superfluity of cholesterol, chocolated
and whip-creamed, hydrogenated
until, in the arteries somewhere, it hardens,
but not now to contemplate such mortalities,
not now a feeling of death or diminishment,
but rather a survey of small abundances,
a log in the fire, a Chopin nocturne
played by Artur Rubinstein or Guomar Novaes,
a Bach cantata, old Elvis tunes, or Tony
Bennett crooning to Bill Evans,
a Schumann *Lied*, perhaps "*Ich Grolle Nicht*,"
sung by Hermann Prey, and, on the stove,
some hot *Glühwein* with cloves and cinnamon,
the scent of a child's popcorn, and,
under the tree-laden temporary greenery,
a cacophony of gifts—stacked, sorted, carded
for their proper recipients—and, outside,

on the grass, a thin encrustation of ice, testimony
to last night's ineffectual incursion of winter
above which, now, in early morning,
a mockingbird salutes from a branch of the yaupon holly
from where he has just evicted a pair of cardinals,
carmine and scarlet in their own way, who have gone
to join the nattering bluejay in a nearby oak,
a mini-menorah of birds, hoping that the minimal oil
of their cries will burn brightly enough to outlast
the mocker's oratory and hunger, as Bill ("William,"
he says, "really") who lives down the road on Merrie Lynn,
stops by to admire our half-finished, fudged, unfilligreed fence,
an urbanite's botched handiwork become suburban,
and our new kitten, L.C., trembles into the first light
of her new abode, a neighborhood filled with streets
named Hemlock, Kern Ramble, Merrie Lynn, Larry Lane,
a melting pot of the leftover and intermarried, the pierced,
poked, tattooed, ever-so-slightly *marginaux* of our local
mini-America, the Erikas and Pauls and Isabelles and Sams,
a Roger Tory Petersonesque amalgam of feathers and pedigrees,
of ever-so-slightly renovated rooms painted in earthtones
and then over-graffitied by children, termites, fire ants,
all things small and beautiful that thrive in this ancestral hotbed
of the mulched and munchable, the compost-driven,
antediluvian upsurge that heats and ferments, that scoops up
from the air an unimaginable abundance, a duff and detritus,
a lustful, free-floating amalgam of untethered dreams
and hopes, a gleeful relinquishment of the moral and moralistic,
a Clintonesque, unimpeachably free-floating libido of aches
and animas, a Freudian and Jungian broth, a flame acanthus

eagerly awaiting its butterflies and hummingbirds,
a millennial overabundance of webs and nets, jujubees
of excess communications e-mailed, faxed and farted out
into real and imaginary time, but brought to earth again
by the soft gurglings of potato water stovetopped somewhere,
the age-old lubricated stops and starts of love and desire,
that old ridiculous harvest of human strivings and ambitions
that ends, finally, when a democratic potato somewhere
finds its way to a flotilla of mouths gathered around a table
and the sweet counterproductivity of crême brûlée melts
once more on the endlessly wagging tongue, reducing it
to the love-hungry vehicle it was meant to be, delicious
with horseradish sauce, or pickled on fresh rye, as is not
befitting this particular season, but delectable nonetheless,
so that the memory of all that is luscious fans out, broadens
the appetite and, at the same time, the sympathy
appetite brings in its delectable wake, so that, no,
friends, this is not a poem whose purpose it is
to overlook the suffering, the sick, the diminished, the deprived,
but only to recognize that we do them no service
when we sentimentalize their pains and pleasures,
when we deprive the world of that sweet abundance
that is sometimes to be taken from it, nor would my friend,
the Hungarian poet Orbán, so unfairly stricken
with Parkinson's disease, want us on his behalf
to abstain from these simple pleasures
which each illness and misfortune only convinces us
are here to be relished; no, he would merely want us
to lift yet another glass of *pálinka* or scotch or cognac or *feher bor*
and give thanks for everything that trembles

on its way in or out of the earth, these splotched,
repainted, reverberating, inhabited, habitable houses
that continue to rotate on the ever-revolving, evolving planet
with their habitations of grace and misery and hunger and love
in God's name and our own, God bless us all.

Sadness

Sooner or later it comes to everyone:
the beautiful prom queen who has lost a breast,
the Don Juan of the tenth grade who has
turned up impotent, the fleet chiropodist
who has developed a limp. Sooner or later it comes,
and you are never prepared for it quite yet,
you who had hoped to be spared through another epoch
of your rightful happiness, you who had always
given to charity. Like a gargantuan tackle
lumbering toward you, it comes and comes,
and—though you may double lateral all you wish,
though you may throw a perfect spiral
up the middle to some ecstatic receiver
and be blessed blue-green some night
by the ministrations of strangers—it will not
spare you. It comes and comes, inevitable
as sunrise, palpable as longing,
and we must go on
laughing it right in the face
until it learns to sing again.

In a Time of Economic Downturn, I Gaze Up at the Sky

The sun came up this morning, just
as I knew it would. My morning coffee
tasted exactly like yesterday's: a tad bitter,
but nonetheless revivifying. The faces
of our dead Presidents on Mount Rushmore,
are still there, speaking of their trials
and tribulations from their scenic outlook
of granite. Tonight, when I get home from work,
my lover will make her way downstairs,
wearing my favorite underwear. We'll lie
in bed, pretending to watch a movie, both
knowing what we really want. The Dow,
no doubt, will continue its slide, just as the moon,
that lozenge of indifference, will continue
on its path downward among the clouds. All of us—
sun, moon, coffee, clouds—might feel a twinge
of guilt: such indifference to profit and loss!
Yet, all over the world, tiny birds with broken wings
and injuries of all sorts are making their way
back to their nests, even the waterlogged anhinga
is drying its wings in the sun. It's good to know
so much keeps going on, despite everything.
Come closer, sweetheart, let's put the film on pause,
let's profit from whatever we've got—before
the closing bell, before the riffraff of recovery
finds us and brings us down again.

The Human Condition

Hard not to wake cheerful
when you can listen to Angela Hewitt playing Couperin
in the morning and the dogwood's blooming
and you have a lover—not a perfect one,
mind you, but it's hardly a world meant
for perfection anyway—and, yes, back pain
of course, high cholesterol, very little socked way
for retirement, but so what? Aphrodisia will
always find its little nooks and crannies, flesh
grows timid and begins to sag with gravity's
insistence, and there are creams, now, for
everything and, for the truly vain, surgery.
For others, like the beautiful actress killed
just this week in a freak ski accident, there's
simply a haphazard life expectancy, not something
we will know about definitively until it happens,
and, wherever it finds us, must celebrate as well.
From the missionary position, all may be sweetness
and light for awhile, but then, all such nonsense aside,
the conviviality of the everyday eventually triumphs,
no matter what happens to AIG and Lehmann.
Birds are all asong in the fir outside, a mass of
foreclosures puckers forth from all sides. Oh
brethren of the mid-range, be with me tonight—
dreams will come again, the good and the bad
of them, and the short sale of the afterlife
will surely garner less than the balance owed,
leaving us free and clear to get on with the future.
Grief, whenever it touches us, should do so

lightly, as should joy. Look out the window:
trees and sky, birdsong and the wild graffiti
of the everyday, just this life and the next one—
out there for the asking like the garbage,
just waiting to be taken away.

"And the Fish Swim in the Lake, and Do Not Even Own Clothing."

—Ezra Pound, "Salutation"

And they never complain, and are never cold,
and their scales shimmer in the sunlight
and their gills flap, their fins perambulate,
they are so trusting of the blessings of water

that their small excursions into air can be nearly lethal
to them, oh dear Saint John the Baptist, you knew of
the blessings of the fish, as did Saint Francis, who also
blessed the birds, and we should rest assured that everything

capable of swimming naked is blessed and ecstatic, so I
rip off my clothes and dive, daily, into the soothing waters
of the Balaton, not an ounce of Hungarian blood in my veins,
but nonetheless Hungarian somehow, a lover of paprika,

pálinka, the fleshy abundance of Hungarian women, air that has
not been rinsed of all its impurities, and these little Balaton carp
and catfish swimming here beside me, they too are counting
their blessings, as is the resilient family of six baby swans

and their vigilant parents, the brown-headed gulls, the clacking storks
nested two to a village, and the stinging underwater nettles, they too
are benedicted by the elements of water, they too are blessed,
though there is no one more sacred than myself here to bless them,

the sunlight shimmering off my goggles, the water purifying,
the air invigorating, then, later, a delicate thin coating of oil
on my skin, the sense that this seemingly self-serving act
has nonetheless accomplished something good for my species,

that I am serving my kind by being here, balls distended and ready
beneath my suit, the day already primed for tumescence, the fish all
naked and oily and lovely in their happy element, as God intended
for all of us to be, though we are not, though there is misery and

poverty and hatred and indifference, but let us not speak of that now,
but only the fish, so naked and oily and happy to be here, so alive.

Gratitude

It's hard to imagine this banana,
having come all the way from Honduras
shaped like a crooked penis
in its yellow winter coat
is here in my hand now
where I am peeling back its foreskin
like a woman (well, you know
what I'm about to say . . .)
and about to eat it, bite
by scrumptious little bite,
progeny of that beautiful red
banana flower, those thick green leaves,
made by the same celestial produce company
that brought us the peach and the grapefruit,
yes, it's hard to believe
that all this has been made purely
for our survival and pleasure,
along, of course, with the monkeys
and other foragers, along with the coconut
and the bright red, South American fruit
known as the *tamate des arboles*, and the jackfruit
and the peach-fuzzy apricot. Yes, I count
this banana among my many blessings,
I am grateful for every little fruit
some forward-thinking Darwinian deity
has made for us, I'm grateful for the plum
and the macadamia nut too, and in the
name of the carnivores among us, those beautiful cows.

Genetics

From my birth mother
I took my melancholy disposition
and from my father
the ability to get through life
with a bullet in one arm.
From my adopted father
a certain way with women
and the ability to sing *"Auf Wiedersehen"*
no matter what the occasion.
From my adopted mother, dead
by the time I was ten, lessons
on tenderness and failed mourning
and from my blind grandmother, Johanna,
the ability to see with my eyes closed
and a strong preference for touch
over appearances. With the help of
my stepmother, the longest survivor of all,
I mastered a difficult course in the damages
the cold heart can sow, and a generous primer
on stinginess. From each one, blood or water,
nature or nurture, I have taken something,
and now, passing on to my own son
God-only-knows what, I am grateful to
all of them, and to my brother Amos, from whom
I inherited a certain cheerfulness, and my sister, Judy,
from whom a tolerance for pain and early death.
I'm even grateful to my cousin Heinz, the baker,
to whom I owe my love of the early morning hours
and to his brother Edgar, from whom—or

at least I hope— I will have received the capacity
for a long and generous life, the need for
a daily swim, and the ability to go
long distances without drowning.

Everyone Is Wonderful When They're Wonderful

The sweet, considerate lover who betrayed you later,
the loving, devoted wife who ran off with your money
and children, the magnificent accountant
who got you the biggest refund of your life and,
shortly thereafter, was arrested for embezzlement,
all of them were wonderful once, weren't they? Why,
even your golf caddy, coming up with just the right club
the day you finally broke par, even the breakfast chef you
were about to fire who, just once, got the poached eggs
and béchamel sauce right, even they reside in your memory,
now, in some glorious afterglow of reality's realness.
*"And YOU, Michael, can be absolutely adorable when you
want to be, which makes me melt . . . and then I can't be angry
at you anymore."* Oh, would it were all so simple, everyone's
best moments their only moments, everyone risen
to the occasions that render them magnificent. Darling,
no doubt, I have been a perfect angel at times, and hope
to be again. But, please, if loving me is what you insist on,
take the whole package for what it is: wonderful
when it's wonderful and then, in equally relevant portions,
Satan himself, cross-dressing a bit for the audience, but still
the same wonderful man who took you to the movies,
merely clad for a different occasion, in different rags,
a different fire burning in the same old heart.

Nostalgia for Paris

I lived in Paris an entire year
between 2003 and 2004, in a
bright lovely flat at 5, *rue Lanneau*
just below the Panthéon, up the hill
from the Boulevard Saint-Germain.
I did all the things Americans in Paris
are supposed to do: I went
for my morning baguette in Saint Michel,
strolled in the *Jardin du Luxembourg*,
visited the zoo in the *Jardin des Plantes*
where Rilke's great poem, "The Panther"
was inspired. I sat on the benches of the
Jardin des Tuileries, watched *les bateaux-mouches*
traversing the Seine. I drank my expresso
at *Deux Magots*, not far from the table
where Sartre sat. I heard Little Jimmy Smith
off the *Rue St. Denis*, read my bilingual Baudelaire,
felt with Rimbaud that life was sometimes *la farce
à mener par tous*. I ate falafel in the Marais,
saw my Rodin, my Picasso too. I had not even one
beautiful lover in Paris, nor even a homely one.
Many nights I traversed *le pont neuf* alone—
there was much to be charmed by in Paris,
that's for sure. But what I remember best of all
is the American Diner on the *Rue des Écoles*,
sitting there Sunday mornings with my son,
dreaming of home, wherever that was.

Poetry Love

It must be wonderful to be so obsessed with poetry
that you live it, breathe it, consider every moment without it

a moment wasted want to do nothing else but write it, read it,
recite it to your friends and lovers it must be wonderful

to have only this one mission for your life, this singular sense
of purpose and pursuit, or perhaps it's terrible, as a friend

once suggested to me over lunch in Cambridge, eating nothing
but ice cream all the time, perhaps it's awful to live on so

restricted a diet even of beauty and pleasure even of language
outgrowing itself I think I might side with those who think

it's terrible this beautiful morning in West Virginia, with the
purple vetch and spring beauties and larkspur and bluebells

blossoming so perfectly, it must be horrible to want to go
perpetually turning everything into poetry to not simply allow

the sacred its moment as the sacred, the profane its tenure
oh one can get so fat from eating too much ice cream,

the arteries clogging, the waistline expanding the breath coming
in shorter and shorter gasps until you die of it, left wishing

you'd at least been able to master the art of prose.

Blessed

The man whose ancestral home has just
burned to the ground in San Bruno, California,
taking with it all his possessions and family memorabilia,
says he is blessed to have found such good friends
to take him in, blessed that his wife and children
have survived with him, he says he is blessed
the way a man who has just given up
his spare kidney feels blessed to have helped a stranger,
the way those thirty-three Chilean miners,
just up from sixty-nine days within the earth's
blackened underbelly, say they are blessed
to see daylight once again, just as most of us,
even without saying so, are blessed, as I am,
this very moment, to receive a postcard from U.S. Army
Captain Scott M. Pastor informing me that my son
has arrived safely at Fort Leonard Wood. (Whoever
would have thought I'd be grateful, even, for *that?*)
Yet who isn't among the blessed, who can still sleep
easily amid the splotched splendors of the quotidian world,
like those 4,500 poor "sufferers" aboard the Carnival
Cruise Line, sentenced to five days of flown-in Spam
and crabmeat and the scent of freshly rotting vegetables?
So much true suffering on this earth, so many
without the balm of other bodies and the beneficence
of breathable air, who have lost the dice-roll of sperm
and egg, or come up with the two of clubs and the three
of diamonds on the blackjack table of this life, down
to their last two chips and final free drink before the time
comes to face the cashier again. Easily the fall air

of West Virginia enters my lungs, easily the day descends
into the solace of sleep and pillows, the *lex loci dilecti*
of misdeeds and small miracles. Grace may not be merited,
friends, but nonetheless deserves to be praised, as I do
now, on this beautiful, unjust, splendiferous earth —
its blessed and bountiful beneficence bouldering down.

ll. Not the Soul

I go to meet that which I liken to . . .

—Jorie Graham, "Soul Says"

Not the Soul

Not, in all likelihood, the soul, with its many rallies,
nor the heart, with its dyspeptic series of fits and starts,
is exactly in charge of us, I fathom, but more likely the sins
of our fathers and the meanderings of our children,
more likely the blessed burdens of our disenfranchisements,
the floating abstractions, the tea breaks and coffee breaks,
the elliptical series of ruinations that await us, and then, even
more likely, our betrayals, the sense of our own sinfulness,
our daily descents into reverie and nightmare, our retroactive
corrections and prospective failures, our unwillingness to barter
what little skills we possess—the embroidered doilies, the
remarkable filigrees—for a small portion of the world's tangible
sanctities. Ah, friends, so many kinds of couscous available
on this very street (*merguez, poulet, agneau, royale,* even *vegetarian*)
and at so many prices, as if the world were, if not our oyster, at least
our couscous—convertible, now, to that single currency
which would make of us all a continent, and then, later, a world,
a signifier signified, like the gull, who at this very moment is
hovering over the roofs here on *rue Thubaneau,* flying over this house,
whooping and laughing, trying to make us change, in the baffling,
now-homogenized currency of extravagance and hope, and of air.

Homage to Hugh Hefner

So many bad things to be said of him:
the brazenly objectified women
the absurdity of that scarecrow body
in its silk pajamas, the soullessness
of much of his sex, the general vulgarity
of everything he stands for. Yet where
in the hearts of most men isn't there
a morsel of envy for someone so brazen
about what he wants, and, what's more,
able to get it? Who among the
badly married or discontentedly tethered
hasn't dreamt of a few nights
in the *Playboy* mansion of his dreams,
all that politically incorrect pleasure,
Jacuzzis-full of beautiful women
fawning over him merely for paying
their bills? Client #9s from every walk of life—
governors, congressmen, vacuum
cleaner salesmen of the world—
which one hasn't, on some failed evening
amid love's vast concordance of harms,
wanted to be him? Old bunny man,
lucky rake, satiated satyr of yesteryear,
so much lubricated pussy and breast
with your silk pajamas and your Viagra
and all that singing to come at your lonely grave.

Samizdat's Muse

He had been writing ambiguous love poems
for so long to his various lovers and wives,
poems with titles like "After Making Love,"

in which the reader could fill in the blanks
as he chose. He had developed a code
for his secret life, one that would endear him

to the faithful and the unfaithful alike,
because he knew that, in the moral world,
there were no absolutes, that language itself

could cut and wound in many ways, no two alike.
So he had become a kind of wall-jumper, someone
who crept through tunnels late at night, and,

now that his work was out there in the world
between covers, he found it was a bit like
Swan Lake under the Communists: never simply

Swan Lake, but, rather, a kind of code,
written in metaphors, understood by each
for his own purposes, late at night, in a country

not entirely of their own choosing.

Civic Leaders

So much virtue in a single room!
The very walls tremble
with the thought of it.
Just think: the weight
of all that goodness!
And such beautiful denials!
Yet everywhere, even here,
life has its way:
somewhere beneath the table
a living hand
reaches out
in search of a knee.

The Germans

Punctual, decent, historically regal,
Their shoes all arranged, their closets in order,
The Germans are reading the *Tagesspiegel.*

One has a schnauzer, the other a beagle,
They walk in the *Grünewald*, father and daughter,
So punctual, decent, historically regal.

The pit bulls are banned now, despised and illegal,
Their masters all outraged, accused of a slaughter,
While placidly reading the *Tagesspiegel.*

It still has its wings spread, that old German eagle,
On statues and monuments, where once there were borders,
Lofty and hovering, historically regal.

Not spendthrift or miserly, nor overly frugal,
Yet burdened by history, darkened by murder,
The Germans are reading the *Tagesspiegel.*

Proud of their Schiller, and proud of their Hegel,
Of Rilke proud too, and of Goethe still prouder,
So punctual, decent, historically regal,
And what are they reading? The *Tagesspiegel.*

Song of the Dow

". . . how easy to be righteous, when you are carefree and rich."
— Cynthia Ozick, "The Impious Impatience of Job"

"Money may not be everything, but it sho lets you act nice."
— Walker Percy, *The Second Coming*

This is a little song in praise of Exxon
and in praise of Xerox and IBM and Microsoft
and, yes, even in praise of Pfizer Chemicals,
the beautiful maker of Viagra,
because they are sweet enough to share in their bounty
because they are the firmament of so many people's naked angels
including my stepmother's, and because not everyone
can be born an instant socialist, with trust funds
and debutante spouses and summers on Martha's
Vineyard and vested annuities. Oh how easy
to be a Marxist, friends, when you've been
papa's little angel, endowed and investitured,
insured and shipped off to the best schools
full of socialist professors and the landed gentry
of high ideals and *Chateauneuf du Pâpe!* But here
among the protean, plebeian, Dow Jones-scouring
masses, there must be someone to sing, too, a song
in praise of Ohio Edison, General Magic, Airtouch
and Ameritech, Mindspring and Ethan Allen—
those magical, patriotic names of money and bottom lines,
those unintended equalizers of risk and dividends.
Oh sweet fathers of Warner-Lambert! Mothers
of Gulfstream and Amazon.com! Why shouldn't I,

who have just invested in the American Italian Pasta Company,
acronym AIPC, press on these delectable keys
in the hope that even Preview Travel will continue to rise,
that the sweet dividends of Lucent and Disney
and Canadian Pacific will continue to make poems like this
possible, that even ECI Telecom will continue to thrive
and, somewhere within the cold bestiary of money,
a splotched angel like myself will not be too timid
to sing of the dollar, the market, the rising, the rallies,
the muse-inspiring beneficence of Texaco, of Cisco,
of Merck and, lest I forget, USA Waste Services.

Virtue

After weeks of a healthy diet, exercise, abstinence
from all forms of sexual activity, he'd had more
than enough of his own piety. The rare hamburger

and onion rings tasted so good, as did the chocolate
cheesecake (in the interests of restraint, he'd said
"no" to the vanilla ice cream) and even the waitress,

not his type in any meaningful sense of the word,
seemed a morsel worth contemplating. After all,
a person could stand only so much of self-

improvement, he thought, it was spring, the dogwoods
were blooming, the Eastern redbuds thrusting a haze
of purple into the air, every once-darkened corner

crying out its possibilities, and what harm could
a little indulgence do on a night like this, after watching
King Lear at the local theatre, when madness,

senility, senescence might be just hours away, when
betrayal, even by one's own body, was a likely
outcome of it all. So, yes, next time he *would* have

that scoop of vanilla ice cream, he *would* have another
Grand Marnier, virtue could wait until morning to
resurrect itself, Gloucester was going to die one way

or another in the end, and honor, though speechless,
needn't be so sanctimonious about itself, tomorrow
was a new tomorrow, he thought, lifting his fork

once more toward his mouth: his hungry mouth,
his ravenous mouth, that God-given mouth made for
eating and swallowing and taking it all bloody in.

Self-Containment

The Helmut Kohl look-alike
in the orange shirt dancing by himself
at this *club échangeiste* must know something

I don't know: He's dancing and dancing,
he's gazing at himself in the mirror
in his pot-bellied splendor, he's smiling

at his own reflection, he seems oblivious
to whether or not he will "score" tonight
or to how expensive the drinks are

or how much he has paid to get here
among the overweight couples and men
with too many buttons unbuttoned, he seems

oblivious to war and peace, injustice and
starvation, he's as captivated as Narcissus by
his own reflection, he's dancing and dancing

and, even when the music changes, the beat
he is dancing to is simply his own, and the
stars in the heavens keep twinkling in vain.

Autobiography of a Face

In memoriam, Lucy Grealy, 1963-2002

You saw your face in mirrors and you cried
to think what fate had done to those like you.
The more you faced your face you had to try

to change the fate that others had applied
to dreams of beauty they had thought were true.
You saw your face in mirrors and you cried

big tears of nightly pain and wounded pride
that neither friend nor surgeon could subdue.
The more you faced your face you wondered why

the less than beautiful are forced to hide,
the shade they're most familiar with: the blue.
You saw your face in mirrors and you cried

for all whose in and out is a divide
between what's mere appearance and what's true.
The more you faced your face you plied

the trade of those who suffer but can't hide
from fates too dark for those as sweet as you.
You saw your face in mirrors and you cried.
You couldn't face your face again, and died.

Desire

Paris, May 2005

Let's just say I seem to be enjoying these three chicken drumsticks
far more than the young man doing sit-ups just across the lawn

beside his girlfriend here at the *Jardin de Reuilly* is enjoying himself:
After all, he's huffing and puffing, and I'm sitting here, devouring

my chicken, basking in the spring sun, but now he's rolling over,
it's push-ups he's doing, push-ups right on top of his girlfriend,

and the push-ups are getting slower and slower, just as my chicken
is disappearing, and, before long, the push-ups stop altogether, he's

merely lying there on top of her, and he seems, even from a distance,
much happier then when he was doing push-ups, then he suddenly

sits up, looks up at the heavens, and stares (with an expression
of pure longing) over at me. *Oh,* he seems to be saying,

I sure wish I had some chicken.

Existential Couplets

1. Rhetorical Question

If love were human nature not a curse
Why, then, would it have fathered so much verse?

2. Posthumous Thoughts of a Mole Beheaded by a Roto-Tiller

I followed my nose, but it didn't seem to know
The places noses aren't supposed to go

3. A Brief History of the Life of Hemingway

He was such a high-romantic figure
Until, at last, he pulled the trigger

4. Hope in Mid-Age

An aging man's hope is that desire
will fizzle out, and not expire

5. The Deaths of Others

The best thing about it, to be blunt,
Is that it's not ourselves who bear the brunt

Of trying hard to breathe from underground
And finding there's no air around

6. On the Relationship between Having Sex Outdoors at Twenty-Eight and Mowing the Lawn at Sixty

The grass was green on both occasions
That's all that links the generations

7. Wisdom at Sixty

It took so long to get, and now it's worth so little
from the darkened vantage of the declining middle

8. Senescence

In youth you heard your elders' counsel, but didn't heed it
Now you see the writing on the wall, and cannot read it

9. "The fact is . . ."

Said by those who seldom know the facts
The mouth asserting what the spirit lacks

10. Satyr

He didn't know a thing, in fact, about the mission
But merely loved its antiquated old position

11. Poets

By the hundreds, by the thousands, night and day
They hunger for the sacred. So it runs away.

12. A Brief History of Sexual Life

The war between domestic life and sex
Goes back to old Tyrannosaurus Rex

Moles

Frantic scribblers beneath the earth
graphomaniacs of dirt and tunnels

mad surrealists, keepers of inexact margins
and stuttering grammar,

I hose down the chapter headings
of your little mounds, I flood you

with the *animus* of the human,
the orderly impulse that loves flat surfaces.

I want to destroy you, keep
my little yard smooth, my grass green.

Wet and blind, you scamper up
from your own sewage

out of the duff and detritus
of your little underground.

Teeny brown Borgeses,
trembling and unsteady,

you struggle toward the nearest shelter,
you burrow back into the dark.

You write on.

III. Be Kind

The Wounded

It is good to pity them
but not too much, or for too long,
lest we make a habit of it
and encourage them to pity

themselves. No, it is best
to apportion our charity
toward some appropriate deserving,
a meritocracy of our own

for there are, after all, so many
spilled waters, so many tragedies
between our first and last utterances
it is best to keep some perspective,

to hold the wounded tenderly
in our arms, then let them go
and try and heal themselves
in any way they can, knowing

they will never entirely be healed,
that, in place of their wounds
there will be scars, phantom pains,
recurrent nightmares, phobias, fears,

a turning away from the place
that wounded them to begin with,
healing though it might prove now.

I myself have been among them.
Pity me. Then stop.

Weeping at the Oscars

Sentimentality, says Stevens,
is failed feeling
and how often I have failed
as I do now
when Charlize Theron comes onstage
to thank her mother for making her
and her make-up man
for making her a *Monster*
and here I go again
crying once more, as I do
every year after the last out
of the World Series
when the players clear the bench
to pounce on the winning pitcher
as I did (three times!) during
The Heart Is a Lonely Hunter
as I will for the rest of my life
in all the wrong places
praising every human victory
over meanness and indecency
no matter how small
weeping for God only knows what.

The Words

If you tell someone you love them
you will give them power
over the sun and moon
you will give them power
over many of your appetites
and how they are satisfied:
over the flowers that decorate your window sill,
even over the contents
of your refrigerator,
you will give them power
over the scent of your sheets
and how often you need to change them
power over the motes of dust
that settle, or fail to,
on certain shelves and night tables
you will give them power
over the color of your socks
power over your very breathing,
its regularities and irregularities,
the missed beats of your heart.
Yes, if you tell someone you love them
there is much to be relinquished,
so very much that your own shoes
will no longer stand still
in their closets, your tissue box
will lie quivering on the night table
awaiting its forthcoming tears.

But things could be worse, I assure you.
If you tell no one you love them
you will give nothing away
and only the air will be left to console you.

Background Music

If you are lucky in love
someone will become the background music
to your own life. She will be there
with you in the same room,
listened to but not actually heard
like a warm hat in winter
and the sounds she makes
will be like a bird's breath
hovering above you
she will be there and not there
at the same time, just as if
you were sitting alone
as if the music were playing
in another room and you
had been dancing only with the walls.

Pancakes

for Jim and Helene Friedberg

My friend Jim has spent a week at my house
and I promise to make him pancakes
before he leaves. I make
very good pancakes, but I happen, alas,
to be out of real maple syrup. *Sorry*, I say,
*there are some things we just have to learn
to live without.* The pancakes are very good
anyway (I've added some flax seed and chai,
soy milk, vanilla yogurt) and Jim seems happy
to share this last breakfast with me, chatting
about our childhoods and our wives, his
overbearing mother and my damaged stepmother,
how we manage to survive pain and somehow,
even, thrive in the face of it. Jim goes upstairs
to pack, he's put the top down on his Mustang
("my mid-life crisis car," he calls it), says
he has one more thing to do before he leaves,
he'll be right back. The thing he has to do
is visit his son Gabe, dead of an overdose
at twenty-two, in the cemetery down the street.
I say I can't imagine the pain of standing
at your child's grave, and he says, yes, there's
this terrible scar tissue and you don't know,
sometimes, how much of it you want to risk
tearing away. Just as he walks out the door,
my wife calls from France. "I couldn't bear it,"
she says, speaking of our only son. "I can't

even bear thinking about it." We hang up
and I begin washing the dishes, just as
Jim walks back in. "Thanks," he says, as I
stare at my reflection in the deep pools
of his eyes, "those pancakes were delicious."

Motel on the Mountain

I remember the sign so clearly
late at night, calling out to me
from the hill off Route 17 West.
Motel on the Mountain
it kept calling, *Motel on the Mountain.*
I was only sixteen,
dreaming of nights of sizzling sex
with my girlfriend Evie
on a king-sized bed
and, when we finally made it there
years later, I remember only
the ersatz Japanese gardens—
water running over stone,
a few lonely cacti and succulents,
I don't even remember
what the sex was like
or the size of the bed
but I will remember all my life
that neon sign calling out to me
below on the highway,
my young hand resting so eagerly
between Evie's bare knees,
Motel on the Mountain Motel on the Mountain—
ode to dreams in the sky and forgotten beds.

The Other Side of the Story

So much to be recounted by so many: how
he betrayed her with his students, and how
she, in turn, tormented him with jealousy;

how there are no solid angels in the world any longer
and how quickly the diaspora of desires spreads,
leaving the hurled stones and disparate narratives

of private intifadas. He was quick to distemper,
she obsessed with the small, domestic details;
he was parsimonious to a fault, she romantic

about all the wonderful things money could buy.
So many evenings had been filled with his tales
of her, hers of him, with both their own innocence

and all those who listened became convinced
of the righteousness of the speaker's version, how
wronged he or she had been in their yarn-spinning self

of virtue and naïveté. Yes, it was so entertaining,
listening to each of them, even the listener himself
could easily forget his own role in the narrative,

that there was always, even now, another side
to the story, to which someone else
at this very moment, was listening, thinking

how the best stories always belong to others,
ever remarkable and entertaining, tales
of good and of evil, almost as true as your own.

Here Is Your Striped Shirt

after Louise Glück

I think now it is better to undress no one
than to undress you. Here is your striped shirt,
the one I bought to hide your furrowed
breasts when you came to bed. I liked
taking it off, I confess, mostly for your arms,
which were ample and fleshy, and because
the feel of flesh against flesh, somehow,
(even with you!) made me happy. I washed it
when you weren't here, and folded it neatly
back into the drawer, where it waited for you
like an old slipper. I tried it on last night—
just in case—but it's way too small. So
I want you to have it back, and your
toothbrush too. You looked
like a prisoner in it anyway.

The Pigeon

Prague, July 2006

Perhaps it was as bored of false praise as I was,
or of lazy language, or maybe it was merely hot
and tired from the summer heat, for when
I returned to my apartment, it was lying there
on the doormat, eyes opened, wings
slightly spread, as if to say it had had enough
of the hot weather, the tourists, the humidity,
(the talking) and there seemed little I could do
beyond pouring some water into a dish
and placing it beside it in front of the door.

It wasn't a day for optimism,
or for high hopes about humanity, so I went
for a nap, hiding myself in the age-old
solace of sleep, far from bad literature
and the spineless flattery concerning it, and
when I woke, some two hours later, went back
to the door. My little dish of water
was the color of tomato juice, the bird's
small head extended, eyes closed, over the edge
and I knew there was nothing more I could do
but empty the syrupy liquid into the toilet bowl,
fold the straw doormat over the stiffened body,
and carry it downstairs.

It landed in the garbage bin with a thud—poor
dead, eloquent thing—and then there was silence,
a profound silence, a deep, wise, beautiful
silence: nothing less, certainly nothing more.

The Past

The Past comes knocking at your door.
It has driven all night from South Carolina
in the rain, eager to see you. The Past
has white hair now, and not much of it.
The Past was pretty once, but no longer:
It has become its own face. The Past would
like to be intimate again, so you must explain,
laboriously, that you are no longer your past—
you are what you are now. And, besides, you
already have two lovers: the Present and Future.
But the Past wants to carry you back to places
you feel blessed to have escaped from. It has come
prepared, with a large collection of memories:
the camping trip to Wellesley Island, Rosenkrantz
and Guildenstern the cats, the unwelcoming parents
and the oversexed sister. The Past meditates twice daily,
reads books with titles like *Deconstructing the Self*,
no doubt a similar self to the one you've worked so hard
to construct. The Past says, *if it gets cold, I'll crawl
into bed with you.* You say to the Past: *Sorry, there's room
for only one in my little bed.* The Past keeps trying
to touch you, the Past likes hugs and deep gazes,
it wants to know all about you. *Oh poor Past,* you say,
what are you doing here? Speak long and hard
to your guru on the phone, pour out your battered
heart. Soon, blessedly, you'll be on your way,
along the highway leading perpetually North.

Say hello to anyone I might have known along the way.
Tell them I no longer have a phone number, not even
an address. Say there's no need to look me up.
Give them all my love.

Self-Help

It was, as it always has been, a choice
between *Twelve Steps to a Compassionate Life*
and *The Story of O*, so I picked up *The Story of O*

knowing it would be more interesting
and, in the long run, better for me. I'd lived
the compassionate life for years — it had proven

far better for those around me than for myself.
Now, I figured, it was time for *The Story of O,*
Tropic of Cancer, Philosophy in the Boudoir, all

the books that had inspired me in my youth,
before altruism gave pleasure a bad name.
We all go back to our origins somehow, I think,

ordering a cappuccino and flirting with the waitress,
probably young enough to be my daughter. Isn't
it, after all, pleasure we truly want, and decency

the back road we use to get there? Why not, rather,
speak our desires straight out, perhaps obliquely,
as in a poem, but nonetheless without shame, so that

pleasure will ultimately reach those who deserve it,
and the books that once gave us so much bad feeling
toward our happier selves can go on doing their work

in the deeply literate darkness underground.

Epithalamium: The Leaves

create love as the leaves
create from the light life

—Robert Duncan

The leaves, in their infinite kindness,
take the light from the air and make it
life. So here, in the sometimes dark,
a hand can be met, a mouth, the fragile
kernels of tenderness we call love
can be scattered over the immaculate hills
until believed. That, too, is kindness.

All loving, a wise man told me, is an act
of finding, a passion to rectify. So here,
in the rectifying air of June, we make right
what we can, leaving the rest as testimony
to its own rightness—the house, the river,
the pontifical clouds hovering like skullcaps
over all your promises.

There are large things we can give to another:
the shared love of light and wind, the grace
of forgiveness, the deep vows whispered here
in the steady shadows of those who believe them.
These words, spoken as if all that there is
in the world could be contained in their sound:

In sickness and in health.
Until the seas part to welcome the planets.

Until the birds have forgotten their beautiful dissonance.
Until the night swallows the sun.

Until light no longer seeks out the leaves
in search of life.

Be Kind

Not merely because Henry James said
there were but four rules of life —
be kind be kind be kind be kind — but
because it's good for the soul, and,
what's more, for others, it may be
that kindness is our best audition
for a worthier world, and, despite
the vagueness and uncertainty of
its recompense, a bird may yet wander
into a bush before our very houses,
gratitude may not manifest itself in deeds
entirely equal to our own, still there's
weather arriving from every direction,
the feasts of famine and feasts of plenty
may yet prove to be one, so why not
allow the little sacrificial squinches and
squigulas to prevail? Why not inundate
the particular world with minute particulars?
Dust's certainly all our fate, so why not
make it the happiest possible dust,
a detritus of blessedness? Surely
the hedgehog, furling and unfurling
into its spiked little ball, knows something
that, with gentle touch and unthreatening
tone, can inure to our benefit, surely the wicked
witches of our childhood have died and,
from where they are buried, a great kindness
has eclipsed their misdeeds. Yes, of course,
in the end so much comes down to privilege

and its various penumbras, but too much
of our unruly animus has already been
wasted on reprisals, too much of the
unblessed air is filled with smoke from
undignified fires. Oh friends, take
whatever kindness you can find
and be profligate in its expenditure:
It will not drain your limited resources,
I assure you, it will not leave you vulnerable
and unfurled, with only your sweet little claws
to defend yourselves, and your wet little noses,
and your eyes to the ground, and your little feet.

IV. No Hurry

Hypochondria

My heart hurts.
My chest hurts.
I'm short of breath.
It could be cancer.
My ejaculation was so small last night—
it must be my prostate.
No one in my family
has lived past the age of seventy:
I turned sixty-nine yesterday.
I forget the name
of the film we saw last night—
it *must* be Alzheimer's.
My vision is failing—diabetes.
Oh God, please help me:
At this rate I'm going
to live forever.

Downhill

You know when the woman leaves
in the middle of the night
and the dog stays
you've reached a point
on the descending slope of the journey
where there's no going back—
a night of halfhearted thrusts
with no climax, snores
that send her homeward before sunrise
and then the relief
of finding yourself alone again
as if you had just gotten off
a chairlift built for two
all by yourself
and were looking down the mountain
at what lies before you
just preparing
to put your skis together
and make your way downhill
without the speed or the elegance
of your younger years
but still moving nonetheless
still taking in the wintry air
shimmying at the hips
kicking up a small spray of snow
when you reach the bottom
and all the while the dog
still waiting for its master in your bed.

No Hurry

for C.K. Williams

This morning waiting for the paint on the fence to dry
I realized there was no hurry, no hurry waiting
for the bus to come no hurry for the sun to set
or the moon to rise no hurry, even, to arrive at orgasm,
your own or anyone else's. There was no hurry,
certainly, for the protoplasm of decline to make its way
homeward, no hurry on the divorce decree no hurry
for the new marriage certificate to arrive no hurry
for the blossoms on the butterfly bush outside this window
to bloom or the apples to fall no hurry for the ant
just now making its way across this room to get to
the other side, though thousands of its little brethren
are impatiently waiting. There was no hurry, I realized,
for these very fingers to make their way over the keys
no hurry for the brave little homunculus of the day
to reach afternoon no hurry for the wrinkles around my eyes
to widen no hurry for impotence bladder problems
mutating cancer cells no hurry, darling, for anything
to become or not become of us no hurry for the plane
to depart *no hurry no hurry no hurry no hurry* since, sooner
or later, we will all arrive at breath's finish line, we will
all be winners, and we will all be still, and everything
we had always been hurrying toward will finally be ours.

I Died

And the day, with its rapt undulations
of hills, no longer spoke to me. Everywhere
a mute, ineloquent silence reigned. It was
winter, icicles distending from the gutters
and treetops, and even if there had been a bird
of paradise in my yard, it was no longer blossoming—
it, too, had entered its latency period. *Underground
underground underground underground* said the wind
and who was I to question its veracity? Surely
there was nothing I had done wrong, but being dead
has a way of silencing the critics, so I simply
stood still, took it all in, thanked whatever gods
there were, and, with a song in my heart
and a prayer on my lips, found all was right
with the world, even if I was no longer part of it,
even if I was dead, and it was evening, and
the next day belonged entirely to others, with me
merely looking on from somewhere else,
somewhere with a life entirely its own.

Two Arts

The art of winning's rather hard to master.
It's easier to lose and blame your fate
for all the things that brought you to disaster.

You lost at poker, then you lost a vaster
fortune that had come your way too late.
The art of winning's rather hard to master.

You try to fill the holes in life with plaster,
then with laughter, sorrow, other kinds of bait
to keep the cards from pointing to disaster.

Your destiny's harsh *frère*, it has a sister,
who scours the world, just looking for a mate,
but winning her is rather hard to master.

The horses run, and yours is running faster
than others gone more quickly out the gate,
and yet you can't help thinking of disaster

in all you do, in every feint and gesture
(in all your jokes, in all your being late).
The art of winning's all too hard to master,
far easier (*oh, God!*) to court disaster.

Two Short

for Isabelle

They'll never be, the other two
that love had made, but life denied
that could have been of me and you.

We were too young, and neither knew
how easily the other cried.
They'll never be, the other two.

So full of purpose gone askew
you came back home, all teary-eyed
to no one else but me and you.

Life turns to life, a yearning stew
that boils and burns and breeds surprise
though they won't be, those other two

that we had made, a witch's brew
of careless love and human pride.
I blame myself, I don't blame you

whose wizened instincts were too few
to summon me to life's good side.
They'll never be, those other two
who could have been of me, and you.

I Think Constantly of Those Who Were Truly Great

and, to be perfectly honest, it bums me out.
So many great ones! — libidinal heroes,
idealists, warrior-chieftains, revolutionaries,
fabulists of all sorts, even the great Irish pig farmers
and Armenian raisin growers — and who,
I ask myself, am I by comparison? Calmed
by Valium, urged on by Viagra, uplifted
by Prozac, I go about my daily rounds,
a quotidian member of the quotidian hierarchy,
a Perseus with neither a war nor a best friend,
and sink to the depths of despair
on the broken wings of my own mundanity.

If only some god had given me greatness,
I surely would have made something of it—
perhaps a loftier, more humble poem than this,
or some *übermenschliche* gesture that would reveal
my superiority to the ordinary beings and things
of this world. But here I am now, one of
the earth's mere Sancho Panzas, leading
those heroic others through the world on their
magnificent horses, merely turning the page, dreaming
my own small deeds into their magnificent arms.

The Nurse

after Tennyson

Now come the purple garments, now the white
Now move the vagrant beds among the disinfected halls
Now stretch the opaque hose between the antiseptic rooms
I waken: and she looks at me.

Now droops the freshly propped-up pillow like a ghost
And like a ghost she sets its right for me.

Now lie the intravenous tubules by the door
And all the body's ills stare openly at me.

Now drifts the slim physician on, and leaves
His clipboard hanging like a thought in front of me.

Now folds the young nurse all her aprons up
And slips her lovely bosom in a waiting car
And so desire folds itself as well, and slips
Into my arms, and then is lost in me.

Abstractions

Events seek them out
and facts
and the names of all those
you have ever known, of every specific bird
in the bramble of every specific tree.

Some are against them
but most frequently those
for whom there's no resonance
when a man in a ditch,
in specific pain, murmurs *justice*
or a young child in Rwanda,
awaiting the specific cold stroke of a macheté,
thinks, in Rwandan: *cruel.*

All those so committedly
against abstraction, it seems,
haven't felt its specific hurts
the way the *fact* of a betrayed heart
seeks the penumbral solace
of like afflictions
until it echoes out
in a few painfully specific syllables.

There's so much to know in the world,
I cry out to those
so in love with their specifics,
until everything we know

issues forth once more
in a few choice abstractions.

Love justice truthfulness hurt,
I say to my workshoppy friends,
in how many ways
would you like me to fill them?
And when I am done with those,
how many specific facts will you
still need, in what shape and size,
and for whose embarrassingly factual sake?

For My Son, Reading *Harry Potter*

How lovely, to be lost
as you are now
in someone else's thoughts
an imagined world
of witchcraft, wizardry and clans
that takes you in so utterly
all the ceaseless background noise
of life's insistent pull and drag soon fades
and you are left, a young boy
captured in attention's undivided daze,
as I was once
when books defined a world
no trouble could yet penetrate
or others spoil, or regret stain,
when, between covers, under covers,
all is safe and sure
and each Odysseus makes it home again
and every transformation is to bird or bush
or to a star atwinkle in some firmament of light,
or to a club that lets you, and all others, in.
Oh, how I wish for you
that life may let you turn and turn
these pages, in whose spell
time is frozen, as is pain and fright and loss
before you're destined to be lost again
in that disordered and distressing book
your life will write for you and cannot change.

Redundancies of Evening

The world is filled with the redundancies
of nighttime: A man who has never kissed another
still says, *Peace, my little friend, your lips*

are soft as apricots in August. But nothing
can make up for the true intimacies of flesh
and fabric, nothing makes us feel better

than the flip and finesse of our finest moments,
when we are lost to our own importance
and gather up the blown petals of flowers,

shake the branches of the mock orange
and refuse to shield our own heads from
what rains down on us. Earthly blessings,

of course, aren't all we're here for;
still, the dark each night brings abates daily,
even the cloudiest skies merely disguise

the inextinguishable light bulb of the sun
lurking behind them. Zinnias will bloom
into late November, the aggrieved will gather

in their tents of fiber and dust, making small fires
even in summer, and whatever I have just said
to you I will doubtlessly say again, without fear

of repeating myself, without, even, the moon
rising once more to whisper sleep.

Homage to Charles Aznavour

*I am at home in my own skin, very much at home even, I am
my own best friend. I always say, "It's too bad a man like me
has to die."*

A man who loves his life may wonder why
the breath that lives and .
Too bad, he thinks, *a man like me must die.*

La joie d'amour, the passionate come-cry
will all be stilled and silenced, like the breath,
and leave the joyful man to wonder why

his passionate regard did not defy
the hovering spirit that provides, and yet
assures that even those who love must die.

The spirit craves eternity, an endless sky
in which the wings of Orpheus have breadth
to soar above the ones who wonder why

the joys of weightlessness are not come by
through trickery, deceit, or mere regret,
but only by the ones who will not die.

And yet such men, as well, must still comply
with laws eternal, never yielding, set.
Too bad, they think, *a man like me must die,*
who loved his life, and now must wonder why.

Anthology

As if in a rest home set beside a cemetery
where the dead far outnumber the living
gaining on them with every page,
first influences, then mentors, then,
most frightening of all, friends
appear and disappear from view,
the rhyming and the unrhymed, the decorous
and decorated, laureates winnowed down
to a handful of their best known and (more rarely still)
their best, from domains public and private
and executors well paid, permissions granted
and occasionally denied, these voices
goading one another on as if
assembled in a house of cards, the first
of which's already down, the rest
now falling, even as they sing and call.

Written on the Day After My Sister's Death

Lake Balaton, Hungary, June 23, 2007

The swan couple, as every year at this time,
are cruising the shore of Lake Balaton
with their seven little ones—
it's always seven, I count each year—
they are looking for crumbs and sandwich bits
from the bathers along the shore
the female out front
the male behind
the young ones between
and they always remind me
of the passing and recurrence of things
as do the storks nesting on my neighbor's chimney
with their infants—
sometimes two, sometimes three—
but always they return from southern climes
and, always again, these births
this familial coherence
that soothes, somehow, beyond ourselves
as today, the late afternoon sun in my face
and the swans perambulating the shore,
I closed my eyes and fell asleep
and when I looked up
they were still there, that family of swans,
making their way toward me
with their seven brown babies—
not six, I counted them again—
but seven still.

For Grief Will Ultimately Have Its Way

is not what I'd like to say to four-year-old
Aaron J. Fisher and his proud young father, here
in the Norfolk YMCA men's locker room, grief

will have its way in love and in the body, it will
have its way, as will disappointment, much
as we'd prefer it to be otherwise. Still, the

pileated woodpecker breeds in the woodlands,
the screech owl prepares to strike from its branches
at dusk, the clacking storks return each summer

to chimneys in Hungarian villages, and wherever
flesh meets, there's still the possibility that
spirit will follow. Soon, we shall sit at our tables

and feast—vegetarians, carnivores, omnivores of every
lust and persuasion, as fickle November looks down
on us, brilliant or inclement as it needs to be, and is.

Who knows where our lust for meaning will take us
eventually? Who knows if our volatile essence can
go on, grasping both ends of the rope at once, seeking

justice *and* the world? *Brief links in the eternal pity,*
a writer once said of us, brief links in the journey
that begins at the table, and ends in the stars. So

bow to the plundered grace of the defeated fowl
that lies before you, bow to the beneficence of fork
and knife. *Smile on,* young Aaron, *smile for everything*

that life can bring you. Grief will ultimately have its
way, that's for certain. So let joy have its way now.

Norfolk, Virginia,
Thanksgiving, 2007

Madden's Pond

Old man Madden's surely dead by now,
and the pond itself overgrown with weeds,
the site of a development or mall,
or just itself, but ordinary now,
a festering stink hole of memory and mud,
though it was once so heavenly to me,
when I would go there with my girl (the girl
I loved then, best I could), our tent, and
our two old cats, Emily and Muir, weekends
after teaching, packed into the little Beetle
we had bought, straight from the factory
that famous summer, 1969, when three men
landed on the moon and Woodstock happened,
and the Isle of Wight, and Kennedy took
Mary Jane Kopechne for a drive (all, it seemed,
in just a matter of days, as if even history itself
could be compressed), but, meanwhile, back
at Madden's Pond, the frogs were jumping
and the crickets wild, with high school students
humping on the grass in summer love and heat,
without remorse, as she and I, too, shook
each other with a passion only youth allows,
and old man Madden fed a young deer on the lawn,
and everything seemed possible and good at
Madden's Pond, which doubtlessly exists no more
though it did then, and Madden too, and love

and possibility and youth and air, still undefeated
and so wholly good, we thought it was eternal,
as we'd like to even now, when ponds are gone
and old men too, and girls, and younger love.

The End of Sex

It was destined to end someday
so why not bow out now, gracefully,
close enough to the top of your game
to remember what it was like? It was,
after all, a lot like life—good at times,
better at others, often disappointing,
on all-too-rare occasions, unforgettable.
Pretty girls had sat on various parts of you—
so *what* if they were pleasuring themselves
elsewhere now? What lay ahead, after all,
were failed performances enhanced by
pharmaceuticals, polite handshakes
after a straight-set defeat. Did *you* really
need to go out in such operatic fashion,
like Nelson Rockefeller (who, the joke goes, came
and went at the same time), or Leonard Warren
in *Il Forza del Destino*? Why, you'd had your day
auf der Bühne, as the Germans say, a better one
than most, and now, whether it was stage door left
or right you exited from, it hardly mattered: Birds
had been in your hand once, and now, no pun
intended, were off somewhere in a bush. And what
was wrong with that? *Let be be finale of seem,*
Stevens said, and why not? You'd already made
your living will: No heroic measures of any kind.
So, girls, take your hands off the old boy's knees:
it'll get you nowhere. Silence may be golden
for the flesh as well. He's happy just to be here,
singing a little song of his own ("No Regrets").

So kiss him one last time, tenderly. And if there's
no heavy breathing in its wake, so be it, and let it
be, and let it have been, and let, if it must, that
sometimes beautiful something never come again.

What Happened?

All you do now is bang on your typewriter during the day and drink in the evening here. What about that powerful third thing, sweetheart? What happened to fornication?

—George Konrád, *A Feast in the Garden*

It fades like embers at late night
after everyone has gone to sleep
the daily need doused
by time's little breezes
and periodic rains
until you wake in the morning
and nothing's burning
though the house still smells
of last night's fires
the dirty dishes
are piled in the sink
and what remains
of last night's feast
is just the scent of it
a mild aftertaste
as if to remind you
how good it tasted
how delectable it must have been.

The Dead

As time passes, you know more and more of them,
the growing community of old friends and neighbors
living, you'd like to think, in the same town, waiting
to welcome you into their midst, perhaps even friends
now themselves. You imagine your friend John Mack
walking down Széchenyi út with your dead Hungarian neighbor
Vera-néni, sharing a *pogacsa*, comparing tales of abductions
and experiments on small ships. You imagine your childhood
best friend, Raymond Fleischhaker, dead of a heart attack
at fifty-eight, having some waffles with your uncle Carl.
Perhaps your aunts Tina and Meta are still playing canasta,
joined at the table by Rima Trop, whom you felt up in a stairwell
after the New York World's Fair, or by Harriet Lieberman,
whose firm brassiere fended off your trembling claws.
Maybe somewhere even your beloved mother Betty
and wicked stepmother Alice are having tea, reminiscing
about the boat trip from Bremerhaven, making jokes about
your father's impotence. You like thinking of the dead as a club,
so democratic in its membership even the good-hearted
and wicked are admitted equally. You like thinking of them
as the last great democracy, everyone with an equal vote,
distributions of income and expenditure so staggeringly just
only a true malcontent, eager to get back to the living,
could complain. Sometimes you see yourself among them,
like someone who has returned to the town of his youth,
moderately successful and tanned, still fit to join
in the revelry of sport and celebration. You unpack your bags,
hang things in the same closets you used as a child, distribute

your toiletries along the top of the dryer. It's just like
old times, you say to yourself, only now there are more of you,
everyone looking far better than you remembered,
everyone washing their faces with the same shining cloth.

Six Cheerful Couplets on Death

Most things won't happen, Larkin said,
But this one will: We will be dead.

The saddest thing, in each context,
Is knowing that we could be next.

Some take the bus, some take the train,
Some die in sleep, the rest in pain

But of one thing we can be sure:
All die imperfect, each impure

Some wishing that they had been better,
Others worse, but no one deader.

Shoes left, like Buddhists, at the door:
Those won't be needed anymore.

God's Window

They are gazing at God's windows.

—Czech proverb describing the easy
indolence of the loafing, vagabond
heroes of Czech folk songs

I sit in the garden listening
to my inner voice. What
could my inner voice be saying?
The birds are singing, says my inner voice,
the storks are nesting. My inner voice
looks up at the sky. *The moon
is waning*, it says, *the sun
is setting.* My inner voice
says nothing about ambition, nothing
about love. *It's been a beautiful day*,
it says, *the moles are tunneling
through the earth.* A scent of honeysuckle
wafts between the trees. *It's getting dark*,
says my inner voice. *It's time
to go to bed.*

About Michael Blumenthal

Photo by Sharon Ryan

Michael Blumenthal is the author of seven previously published books of poetry, the novel *Weinstock Among the Dying*, and the memoir *All My Mothers and Fathers*, among other books. Formerly Director of Creative Writing at Harvard, he is currently Visiting Professor of Law at the West Virginia University College of Law and lives in Morgantown, West Virginia, and Hegymagas, Hungary.

Books from Etruscan Press

Zarathustra Must Die | Dorian Alexander
The Disappearance of Seth | Kazim Ali
Drift Ice | Jennifer Atkinson
Crow Man | Tom Bailey
Coronology | Claire Bateman
Cinder | Bruce Bond
Peal | Bruce Bond
Toucans in the Arctic | Scott Coffel
Body of a Dancer | Renée E. D'Aoust
Nahoonkara | Peter Grandbois
Confessions of Doc Williams & Other Poems | William Heyen
The Football Corporations | William Heyen
A Poetics of Hiroshima | William Heyen
Shoah Train | William Heyen
September 11, 2001, American Writers Respond | Edited by William Heyen
As Easy As Lying | H. L. Hix
Chromatic | H. L. Hix
First Fire, Then Birds | H. L. Hix
God Bless | H. L. Hix
Incident Light | H. L. Hix
Legible Heavens | H. L. Hix
Lines of Inquiry | H. L. Hix
Shadows of Houses | H. L. Hix
Wild and Whirling Words: A Poetic Conversation | Moderated by H. L. Hix
Art Into Life | Frederick R. Karl
Free Concert: New and Selected Poems | Milton Kessler
Parallel Lives | Michael Lind
The Burning House | Paul Lisicky
Synergos | Roberto Manzano
The Gambler's Nephew | Jack Matthews
Venison | Thorpe Moeckel
So Late, So Soon | Carol Moldaw
The Widening | Carol Moldaw
White Vespa | Kevin Oderman
The Shyster's Daughter | Paula Priamos
Saint Joe's Passion | JD Schraffenberger
Lies Will Take You Somewhere | Sheila Schwartz
Fast Animal | Tim Seibles

American Fugue | Alexis Stamatis
The Casanova Chronicles | Myrna Stone
White Horse: A Columbian Journey | Diane Thiel
The Fugitive Self | John Wheatcroft

Etruscan Press Is Proud of Support Received From

Wilkes University

Youngstown State University

The Raymond John Wean Foundation

The Ohio Arts Council

The Stephen & Jeryl Oristaglio Foundation

The Nathalie & James Andrews Foundation

The National Endowment for the Arts

The Ruth H. Beecher Foundation

The Bates-Manzano Fund

The New Mexico Community Foundation

Gratia Murphy Fund

Founded in 2001 with a generous grant from the Oristaglio Foundation, Etruscan Press is a nonprofit cooperative of poets and writers working to produce and promote books that nurture the dialogue among genres, achieve a distinctive voice, and reshape the literary and cultural histories of which we are a part.

etruscan press
www.etruscanpress.org

Etruscan Press books may be ordered from

Consortium Book Sales and Distribution
800.283.3572
www.cbsd.com

Small Press Distribution
800.869.7553
www.spdbooks.org

Etruscan Press is a 501(c)(3) nonprofit organization.
Contributions to Etruscan Press are tax deductible
as allowed under applicable law.
For more information, a prospectus,
or to order one of our titles,
contact us at books@etruscanpress.org.

Printed in the USA
CPSIA information can be obtained
at www.ICGtesting.com
LVHW090805080824
787695LV00003B/380